8500001

PROPERTY OF
Capt. Isaac Paine
ELEMENTARY SCHOOL
LIBRARY

Claude Monet

BY KATHERINE KRIEG • ILLUSTRATED BY J.T. MORROW

Published by The Child's World®
1980 Lookout Drive • Mankato, MN 56003-1705
800-599-READ • www.childsworld.com

Acknowledgments
The Child's World®: Mary Berendes, Publishing Director
Red Line Editorial: Editorial direction and production
The Design Lab: Design

Photographs ©: Claude Monet, cover, 1, 4–5, 7, 11, 13, 14, 17, 19 (top left), 19 (top right), 19 (bottom), 21; Étienne Clémentel, 6; Christie's Images/Corbis, 9; Bridgeman Art, 15; Bensliman Hassan/Shutterstock Images, 16–17; Nadar, 20

Copyright © 2015 by The Child's World®
All rights reserved. No part of this book may be reproduced or utilized in any form or by any means without written permission from the publisher.

ISBN 9781626873483
LCCN 2014930687

Printed in the United States of America
Mankato, MN
November, 2014
PA02252

ABOUT THE AUTHOR

Katherine Krieg is a writer and art enthusiast. She has seen a collection of Monet's haystack paintings at an art museum.

ABOUT THE ILLUSTRATOR

J.T. Morrow has worked as a freelance illustrator for more than 25 years and has won several awards. His work has appeared in advertisements, on packaging, in magazines, and in books. He lives near San Francisco, California, with his wife and daughter.

CONTENTS

CHAPTER 1

An Impressionist 4

CHAPTER 2

Childhood and Beginnings 8

CHAPTER 3

A New Movement 12

CHAPTER 4

An Artist's Home. 18

Glossary 22

To Learn More 23

Index 24

CHAPTER 1
An Impressionist

Claude Monet was a French artist. Monet painted many outdoor scenes using loose brushstrokes. He was one of the first **Impressionists**. Impressionism was a new art style.

In the 1800s, French people liked art made by artists who had gone to special art schools. These were called **academic** artists. Their art was usually realistic, looking like real life. It often showed scenes from history or the Bible. An annual Salon, an **exhibition** of art, showed popular academic art.

But Monet and his friends wanted to make different art. They did not like academic art. They wanted to paint the things they saw around them. They often painted nature and **landscape** scenes. They would be called Impressionists. The art movement they started would be called Impressionism.

Impressionists also used brighter colors. Sometimes

> **IMPRESSIONISM AND COLOR**
> *Color is an important part of a painting. Color can be used to create shadows and depth. It can change the feeling of a work. Academic artists usually used dark colors, such as gray and black, to make shadows. But Impressionists used brighter colors, including blues, greens, and yellows.*

the colors were not blended well on the **canvas**. Sometimes the brushstrokes were visible on the paper. Academic artists carefully planned out a painting before they started. But most Impressionists claimed not to do this. They wanted to create art freely.

Monet and the other Impressionists used bright colors.

At first, most people did not like the new style. Some thought the paintings looked unfinished. But Monet didn't care. He thought the new style was better than the old.

Because Impressionism was not popular at first, Monet could not sell his paintings. Monet had very little money. He struggled to feed his family. But he always stayed true to his art.

Finally, by the late 1890s, people in the United States became interested in Impressionism. Monet's hard work was

Monet in his garden, 1917

finally understood. By 1900, people in France had caught on to the trend. Monet became famous for his paintings—art that had been disliked just years earlier.

Monet knew how he wanted his art to look. Even though many people didn't like it at first, Monet continued doing what he loved. Today, his paintings are some of the most famous in the world.

The Japanese Bridge *shows the bridge in Monet's garden.*

CHAPTER 2

Childhood and Beginnings

Claude Monet was born on November 14, 1840. His family lived in Paris, France. In 1845, they moved to Le Havre. This town was north of Paris. It was closer to the ocean.

In 1851, ten-year-old Claude started taking drawing classes in school. Claude took some classes with Jacques-François Ochard, a local artist. As a teenager, Claude drew cartoons. He used charcoal and paper. Claude drew funny **caricatures** of people he knew. He even drew caricatures of his teachers. Claude sold some of his drawings to people in town.

When Claude was 16 years old, his mother died. Around this time, Claude left school. He started to focus on art.

Claude met local artist Eugène Boudin. Boudin often painted nature scenes. He was interested in how the same scene looked different depending on the weather or light. Claude started doing landscape paintings like Boudin. He enjoyed painting outside as Boudin did. But he thought Boudin's work looked too realistic.

His head is so big!

Many of Monet's caricatures showed people with funny, big heads.

In April 1859, Monet moved to Paris. He wanted to be a painter. He went to an art **academy** there. He also made friends with other artists. When he was 22, Monet became a student of artist Charles Gleyre.

Monet and Gleyre's other students experimented with new types of art. Academic artists painted scenes that looked realistic. But Monet and the other students were trying new things. They often painted outside. They used quick brushstrokes. This gave their paintings a more flowing, less exact look.

Monet sent in two paintings, *The Woman in the Green Dress* and *Forest of Fontainebleau*, to the 1866 Salon. The Salon was a yearly exhibit of artwork in Paris. Both of Monet's paintings were accepted.

Monet's *The Woman in the Green Dress* shows a new style developing. He used dark colors, which were common in **traditional** portraits. But, unlike the old style, Monet **posed** his **model** in a position common for magazine models. He also painted her wearing popular, trendy clothing of the time.

Monet was just beginning to challenge popular art. And, with his work in the 1866 Salon, he was on his way to becoming a great artist.

PLEIN-AIR PAINTING

As a young artist, Monet became interested in plein-air painting. Plein air means "open air" in French. This means that the artist paints outside. Plein-air artists often paint landscapes. But they may paint people and other things they see outside. Many painters still enjoy this approach today.

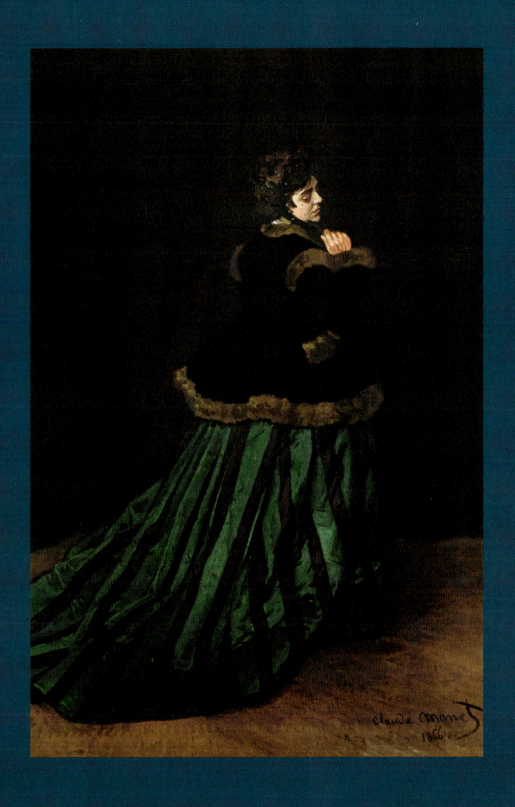

The Woman in the Green Dress *was accepted by academic artists, but it shows how Monet's style was changing.*

CHAPTER 3

A New Movement

Monet continued to get his work in the Salon. But sometimes his work was rejected. Monet spent a lot of time creating *Women in the Garden.* He dug a trench in the garden so he could paint from the right angle. He raised and lowered his canvas with a pulley. But the 1867 Salon didn't want it.

Paintings of women in gardens were a common subject. But Monet's painting was different. The brushstrokes were easy to see. People liked paintings that hid the brushstrokes better. Most people expected a painting to tell a story. But in *Women in the Garden,* the story was not easy to see. The women wore modern clothes. It confused people.

Monet struggled to support himself with his paintings. Monet's lack of money was a problem. He was a expecting a baby with his girlfriend, Camille Doncieux. Camille was the

> **MODELS**
> *Artists often use models when they are painting images of people. Models sometimes have to stand very still while an artist paints them in a certain pose. In* The Woman in the Green Dress, Women in the Garden, *and many other paintings, Monet used Camille as his model. For this reason, the women in* Women in the Garden *look alike.*

Women in the Garden *confused art critics at the time.*

model for many of Monet's paintings. She was all three women on the left in *Women in the Garden*.

In the summer of 1867, Monet went to live with his aunt to save money. He had to leave Camille in Paris. Monet and Camille had a son, Jean, on August 8, 1867. Monet visited Paris to see the baby. In 1870, Monet and Camille married. But that same year, a war broke out in France. To stay out of the fighting, Monet moved to England. He spent a year there painting what he saw. Then, he returned to Paris.

In 1874, Monet and his artist friends created a club. It was called the Anonymous Society of Painters, Sculptors, and Printmakers. Monet and his artist friends held their

Monet painted The Thames below Westminster *in England.*

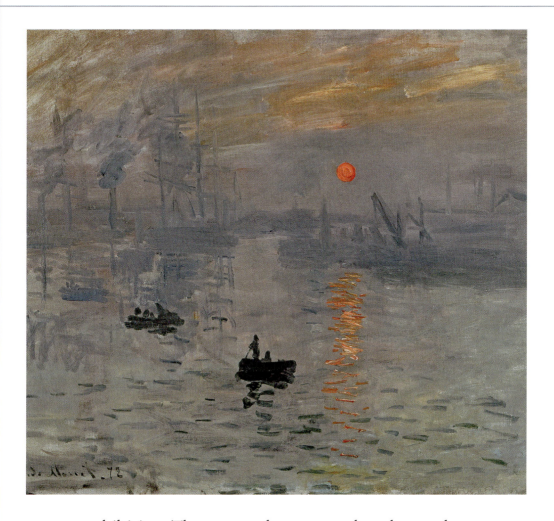

own exhibition. They wanted more people to know about their art.

Monet had several works in the show. One of these works was *Impression, Sunrise*. Many people made fun of Monet's painting. They thought his paint strokes looked sloppy. Some said the painting looked unfinished.

But Monet was glad for the **criticism**. He wanted his art to be different. People started calling Monet and his friends

Monet dabbed paint on the canvas using quick brushstrokes in Impression, Sunrise.

Impressionists after Monet's painting. An impression can be quick and unfinished. It was meant to be an insult. But Monet and the other artists welcomed the name. Together they'd started a new art movement—Impressionism.

In 1876, Monet met Ernest Hoschedé and his wife, Alice. The Monets and the Hoschedés became good friends. They decided to move with their families to the small town of Vétheuil, near Paris. The two families lived in a house together.

Monet continued to paint in Vétheuil. But Camille got sick. She had the couple's second child, Michel, on March 17, 1878. Then on August 5, 1879, Camille died.

Monet started to have money problems again. But he continued to paint his vision. He hoped it would lead to something.

Monet painted his View of Vétheuil *in 1880 during his time in the village.*

CHAPTER 4
An Artist's Home

After the death of his wife, Monet and his two sons kept living with the Hoschedés. Monet and Alice fell in love. When Alice's husband lost all his money, he left France. Monet and Alice moved to Paris together. They lived with Monet's sons and Alice's six children. Alice helped raise Monet's children.

Monet was also starting to hear good things about his art. Americans learned of Monet in the 1880s. Many people in the United States liked his art. U.S. art collectors began to buy more of his paintings.

Also during this time, Monet started to paint series paintings. He would paint the same thing several times for different paintings. He might do one painting in the morning. Then, he'd do another of the same subject during the sunset. Monet wanted to show how things looked different at different times of the day.

OTHER IMPRESSIONISTS
Monet was just one of many popular Impressionist painters. Some of the most famous are Édouard Manet, Pierre-Auguste Renoir, and Edgar Degas. The French Impressionists knew each other. Sometimes they even bought each other's art.

In one series, Monet painted **haystacks**. *Haystacks (Effect of Snow and Sun)* is one of these paintings. In this painting, Monet was paying attention to light. He shows the shadows of haystacks. Sometimes Monet had to hurry to finish a painting before the light changed.

Monet's Haystacks (Effect of Snow and Sun), top left, *is one of several in the series, including* Haystacks (Sunset), top right, *and* Haystacks (Midday), bottom.

In April 1883, Monet, Alice, and their family moved to a house in Giverny. Giverny is a town northwest of Paris. After her husband died, Alice married Monet in 1892.

Monet planted large gardens outside the house in Giverny. He painted water lilies and other plants in the garden. These became some of his best-known paintings.

In 1899, Monet painted *Bridge over a Pond of Water Lilies*. It was one of a series of paintings of this bridge. In these paintings, Monet continued to experiment with light. He also focused on how light reflected off the pond.

Bridge over a Pond of Water Lilies was also different from common landscape paintings. Most landscapes have a **horizon** line. This is usually where the ground meets the sky. Monet's painting had no horizon.

By 1900, Monet's own country was starting to see his talent. Impressionism had finally become popular in France. Monet and his work became famous.

As Monet grew older, his eyesight got worse. On December 5, 1926, Monet died from lung cancer. He had painted all his life. He was 86 years old.

Monet's impact on the art world lives on. His work is still loved today. Monet was an artist who bravely broke the rules and started a movement.

Monet's Impressionist style helped pave the way for new styles of art in the 1900s.

Bridge over a Pond of Water Lilies *was one of many paintings Monet made of his gardens.*

Glossary

academic (ak-uh-DEM-ik) Something academic has to do with school or learning. Academic artists studied classic art.

academy (uh-KAD-uh-mee) An academy is a secondary school. Monet briefly attended an art academy in Paris.

canvas (KAN-vuhs) A canvas is a heavy cloth on which a painting is made. In Monet's paintings, the paint was often not well blended on the canvas.

caricatures (KAR-i-kuh-chers) Caricatures are humorous depictions of people or things. As a teenager, Monet drew caricatures of his teachers.

criticism (KRIT-i-si-zum) Criticism is expressing disapproval or noting the faults of something. Monet received criticism for his new style of work.

exhibition (ek-suh-BISH-uhn) An exhibition is a public display of work. Monet and his friends held their own art exhibition.

haystacks (HEY-staks) Haystacks are bound piles of hay. Monet painted haystacks under different types of light.

horizon (huh-RHY-zuhn) A horizon is the place where the ground appears to meet the sky. Some of Monet's landscape paintings have no horizon.

Impressionists (im-PRESH-uhn-ists) Impressionists were French painters of the late 1800s who formed a new style of art. Monet and other Impressionists used bright colors in their paintings.

landscape (LAND-skeyp) A landscape is a large area of land that can be seen in one view. Monet and other Impressionists often painted landscapes.

model (MOD-ul) A model is a person who serves as the subject for a work of art. Monet's wife, Camille, often served as his model.

posed (pohzd) Someone who posed held a position to be painted or drawn. Camille posed for many paintings for Monet.

traditional (truh-DISH-uhn-uhl) Traditional relates to a custom or idea that has been passed down through the years. Monet did not want to paint in traditional styles.

To Learn More

BOOKS

Maltbie, P. I. *Claude Monet: The Painter Who Stopped the Trains*. New York: Abrams Books for Young Readers, 2010. Print.

Waldron, Ann. *Who Was Claude Monet?* New York: Grosset & Dunlap, 2009. Print.

Wood, Alix. *Claude Monet*. New York: Windmill, 2013. Print.

WEB SITES

Visit our Web site for links about Claude Monet:
childsworld.com/links

Note to Parents, Teachers, and Librarians:
We routinely verify our Web links to make sure they are safe and active sites. So encourage your readers to check them out!

Index

academic artists, 4–5, 10

Boudin, Eugène, 8
Bridge over a Pond of Water Lilies, 20
brushstrokes, 4, 5, 10, 12

cartoons, 8
color, 4

Doncieux, Camille, 12, 14, 16

Forest of Fontainebleau, 10

Gleyre, Charles, 10

Haystacks, 19
Hoschedé, Alice, 16, 18, 20
Hoschedé, Ernest, 16, 18

Impression, Sunrise, 15
Impressionism, 4, 6, 16, 20

landscapes, 4, 8, 10, 20

Monet, Claude
   childhood, 8
   children, 14, 16, 18
   creating Impressionism, 15–16
   death, 20
   marriages, 14, 20
   money problems, 6, 12, 16, 18

Ochard, Jacques-François, 8

Paris, 8, 10, 14, 16, 18, 20
plein-air painting, 10

Salon, 4, 10, 12

Woman in the Green Dress, The, 10, 12
Women in the Garden, 12, 14